I0016519

DIALOGUE WITH DIGITAL MINDS:
YOUR GUIDE TO CHATGPT

ONESIMUS MALATJI

Dialogue with Digital Minds: Your Guide to ChatGPT

By: Onesimus Malatji

DIALOGUE WITH DIGITAL MINDS:

YOUR GUIDE TO CHATGPT

ACKNOWLEDGMENTS

I extend my deepest gratitude to everyone who has been a part of this incredible journey, both seen and unseen. Your support, encouragement, and unwavering belief in me have been the driving force behind the creation of this book.

To my family, for standing by me through thick and thin, for believing in my dreams, and for being a constant source of inspiration – your love and encouragement have been my guiding light.

To my friends, mentors, and colleagues, your valuable insights and feedback have shaped the ideas within these pages. Your willingness to share your wisdom and experiences has enriched this work beyond measure.

To all those who have supported me on my path, whether through a kind word, a helping hand, or a moment of shared understanding, thank you. Your presence in my life has made all the difference.

To the countless individuals who have faced challenges and setbacks, yet continued to strive for greatness, your stories have fuelled the inspiration behind these words. May you find solace and encouragement within these pages.

And finally, to the readers who have embarked on this journey with me, thank you for allowing me to share my thoughts and experiences. It is my hope that this book serves as a beacon of hope, a source of guidance, and a reminder that fulfilment can be found in every step of life's intricate tapestry.

With heartfelt appreciation,

Onesimus Malatji

DEDICATION

Being one of the difficulties in my family, always stubborn, I thank God I turned out alright. I dedicate this book to my mother, Esther Malatji. I will always love you. You have raised me well until I became a fully grown man. Thank you for your prayers and support during my tough times in life. Additionally, I extend my heartfelt dedication to my family, Thank you. I love you so much.

TABLE OF CONTECT **PAGES**

DIALOGUE WITH DIGITAL MINDS:
YOUR GUIDE TO CHATGPT

INTRODUCTION TO CHATGPT: UNDERSTANDING AI CONVERSATIONS

In the ever-evolving landscape of technology, the emergence of artificial intelligence (AI) has marked a significant milestone in how humans interact with machines. At the forefront of this AI revolution is ChatGPT, a tool that is redefining our approach to AI conversations. This chapter aims to introduce you to the world of ChatGPT, offering a foundational understanding that will serve as a stepping stone to more advanced interactions and applications.

To appreciate the significance of ChatGPT, it's important to understand the broader context of conversational AI. Historically, human interaction with computers was limited to specific commands and rigid programming.

The evolution of AI, particularly in the field of natural language processing (NLP), has broken down these barriers, enabling machines to understand and respond to human language in a way that is both intuitive and remarkably human-like.

ChatGPT, developed by OpenAI, stands as a testament to the advancements in NLP. It is an AI language model designed to generate human-like text based on the prompts it receives.

What sets ChatGPT apart is its ability to engage in conversations, answer questions, and even create content that ranges from poetic verses to technical manuals, all with a level of coherence and relevance that was once the sole domain of human intellect.

At its core, ChatGPT is built on a type of AI known as a transformer model, which is trained on vast amounts of text data. This training enables the model to learn patterns in language, understand context, and generate responses that are not just accurate but also contextually appropriate. The beauty of ChatGPT lies in its machine learning capabilities; it's not just coded with fixed responses but rather learns and adapts from the input it receives, making each interaction unique.

One of the key features of ChatGPT is its ability to maintain context in a conversation. Unlike earlier AI models that treated each interaction as standalone, ChatGPT can remember and reference previous parts of the conversation, lending a sense of continuity and understanding that is crucial for meaningful dialogue.

The potential applications of ChatGPT are vast and varied. From assisting with customer service inquiries to aiding in creative writing, ChatGPT is proving to be a valuable tool across numerous fields. Its ability to process and generate language has opened doors to applications that were previously unfeasible with traditional programming methods.

As we embark on this journey to understand and utilize ChatGPT, it is important to recognize both its capabilities and its limitations. Like any technology, ChatGPT is a tool, and its effectiveness depends on how it is used. This chapter sets the stage for a deeper exploration of ChatGPT, laying the groundwork for you to harness its potential in the most effective way.

THE EVOLUTION OF CHATGPT: A BRIEF HISTORY

The journey of ChatGPT is an integral part of the broader narrative of artificial intelligence, particularly in the realm of natural language processing (NLP). This chapter takes you through the key milestones and developments that have led to the creation of ChatGPT, illustrating the remarkable evolution of conversational AI. In the mid-20th century, the early efforts in NLP were centred around rule-based systems. These systems, limited by their inability to adapt to the nuances and complexities of human language, marked the initial attempts at creating machines that could mimic human conversation.

The introduction of machine learning in NLP brought about a significant change. Moving away from the confines of rule-based systems, machine learning models learned language patterns from extensive text data, allowing for more adaptive and nuanced interactions with machines.

The transformer model, unveiled in 2017, revolutionized NLP. This model processed words in relation to each other within a sentence, vastly improving the understanding of context. This innovation was a key stepping stone in the development of advanced language models, paving the way for ChatGPT.

The Generative Pre-trained Transformer (GPT) series, developed by OpenAI, marked a new era in AI. Starting with GPT and evolving through GPT-2 and GPT-3, these models demonstrated an unprecedented ability to generate coherent and contextually relevant text. They formed the technological foundation upon which ChatGPT was built.

ChatGPT, a specialized iteration of the GPT series, emerged with a unique focus on conversational interaction. Fine-tuned to interact more humanly, ChatGPT showed an enhanced ability to maintain context and manage dialogues, significantly advancing the field of conversational AI.

The impact of ChatGPT has been widespread, touching various sectors from education to customer service. Its capability to generate human-like text has not only improved user experiences but also opened new avenues in automating complex, language-dependent tasks.

The history of ChatGPT reflects the continuous journey of AI and NLP. From simple rule-based systems to the sophisticated, context-aware capabilities of ChatGPT, this evolution underscores the rapid advancements in AI and sets the stage for future innovations in human-AI interactions.

HOW CHATGPT WORKS: BEHIND THE AI TECHNOLOGY

Delving into the mechanics of ChatGPT reveals a fascinating blend of advanced artificial intelligence technologies. This chapter aims to unravel the complexities behind ChatGPT, offering a clear understanding of the AI technology that powers its conversational abilities.

At the core of ChatGPT's functionality is the transformer model, a revolutionary neural network architecture that has significantly advanced the field of natural language processing (NLP). Unlike earlier models that processed text linearly, transformers handle entire blocks of text in parallel, enabling a more profound understanding of context and nuances in language.

The effectiveness of ChatGPT hinges on two critical processes: pre-training and fine-tuning. During pre-training, the model is exposed to a large corpus of text data, learning the intricacies of language patterns, grammar, and style. This stage is not task-specific; rather, it allows the model to develop a comprehensive language base. The fine-tuning phase tailors the model to specific tasks, in this case, conversational patterns, optimizing its ability to interact in a dialogue setting.

A remarkable feature of ChatGPT is its dual capability to comprehend input text and generate coherent, contextually relevant responses. This is achieved through a method called 'masked language modelling' used during training, which teaches the model to predict and fill in missing parts of text, enhancing its grasp of context and semantics. This capability forms the backbone of ChatGPT's conversational prowess.

One of the significant challenges in conversational AI is managing context and memory throughout an interaction. ChatGPT addresses this by retaining and referencing information from earlier parts of the conversation, thus maintaining a continuous and relevant dialogue flow. However, there are limitations to this memory capacity, which impact the extent of context retention in a single interaction.

Developing ChatGPT also involved addressing ethical and safety concerns. Efforts were made to reduce biases and prevent the generation of inappropriate content. This involves both technological measures in the model's design and ethical guidelines in its application.

Finally, it's important to recognize that ChatGPT is part of an evolving landscape of AI technologies. Continuous research and development efforts aim to enhance its capabilities, refine its conversational skills, and broaden its application spectrum.

In understanding how ChatGPT works, we gain not only an appreciation for its current abilities but also an insight into the potential future developments in AI-driven conversational tools. This knowledge sets the foundation for exploring practical interactions with ChatGPT and leveraging its capabilities in various domains, as discussed in the upcoming chapters.

SETTING UP FOR SUCCESS: PREPARING TO USE CHATGPT

Embarking on the journey of using ChatGPT requires a blend of technical preparation and strategic planning. This chapter aims to guide you through the initial steps necessary to effectively utilize ChatGPT, ensuring that you have a solid foundation for your interactions with this advanced conversational AI.

The very first step involves understanding the technical requirements to access ChatGPT. Most commonly, ChatGPT is available via a web-based platform or an API, necessitating a reliable internet connection and a compatible device, such as a computer or smartphone. Ensuring your technology aligns with these requirements is crucial for a seamless ChatGPT experience.

For many ChatGPT services, creating an account is the gateway to access. This process typically involves providing basic personal information and agreeing to certain terms of use. Paying attention to these terms is important, as they delineate your permissible scope of activities, potential costs, and any usage limits.

Once access is secured, acquainting yourself with the ChatGPT interface is your next step. Take time to explore how to input prompts, interpret responses, and, if available, customize your settings.

An intimate understanding of the interface enhances not only the efficiency but also the enjoyment of your interactions. Having clear objectives for your use of ChatGPT can significantly enhance the experience. Whether your goals are educational, professional, recreational, or creative, understanding what you want to achieve helps in crafting effective prompts and directing your interactions more purposefully.

The art of prompting is central to getting the most out of ChatGPT. Beginning with simple questions and gradually moving to more complex ones is a practical approach. This process allows you to observe how the AI responds to different types of prompts and how subtle variations in language can influence the outcomes.

Privacy and data security are paramount considerations. When interacting with ChatGPT, be cautious about sharing personal or sensitive information and stay informed about the data handling practices of the platform you're using.

Exploring the various applications and use cases of ChatGPT can provide valuable insights into its capabilities. ChatGPT's utility spans a broad spectrum, from answering simple queries to assisting in complex tasks like creative writing, programming, or even language translation.

Lastly, staying abreast of the latest updates and understanding the evolving capabilities and limitations of ChatGPT is crucial. As AI technology continues to advance, being informed helps you adapt your usage strategies and manage your expectations.

By following these guidelines, you'll be well-prepared to navigate the world of ChatGPT effectively. As we progress through the book, the upcoming chapters will delve into more detailed techniques and insights for interacting with ChatGPT, further enhancing your ability to leverage this innovative tool across various scenarios.

THE BASICS OF CRAFTING PROMPTS

Mastering the art of prompt crafting is essential for effective communication with ChatGPT. This chapter focuses on the foundational principles that guide the creation of prompts, ensuring clarity, relevance, and precision in your interactions with this sophisticated AI tool.

The essence of prompt crafting lies in how you communicate your needs or inquiries to ChatGPT. A prompt can be as simple as a direct question or as complex as a request for creative generation, but its formulation significantly influences the AI's response.

Clarity and specificity are paramount in prompt crafting. The clearer and more specific your prompt, the more likely you are to receive a relevant and accurate response from ChatGPT. Vague or ambiguous prompts often lead to less precise responses, which may not align with your expectations or requirements.

Including contextual information in your prompts is highly beneficial, particularly for complex queries. By providing background or situational details, you enable ChatGPT to understand the framework of your request, resulting in responses that are more tailored to your specific scenario.

The length and detail of your prompt also play a critical role. While longer prompts can offer more context and clarity, it's important to strike a balance. Overly lengthy or detailed prompts might cause the core of your request to become diluted, potentially leading ChatGPT away from the intended focus. On the other hand, excessively brief prompts may lack the necessary information for ChatGPT to grasp the full extent of your request, leading to generalized or off-target responses.

Effective prompt crafting also involves anticipating how ChatGPT might interpret your words. It's helpful to think from the AI's perspective, considering the potential ways it might process and respond to your prompt. This mindset encourages you to refine your prompts to align more closely with how ChatGPT operates, enhancing the likelihood of receiving the desired outcome.

Another aspect of prompt crafting is iterative refinement. Often, the first response from ChatGPT may not fully meet your needs. In such cases, refining and adjusting your prompt based on the initial response can guide the AI towards a more accurate and relevant output. This iterative approach is particularly useful for complex or nuanced requests where the first attempt may not immediately yield the perfect result.

Lastly, understanding the limitations of ChatGPT is crucial in setting realistic expectations for its responses. Recognizing that ChatGPT may not always provide the desired answer or may have limitations in understanding certain contexts helps in formulating prompts that are within the AI's scope of capability.

By adhering to these fundamental principles, you can craft effective prompts that facilitate meaningful and productive interactions with ChatGPT. As you become more familiar with these basics, you'll be well-equipped to explore more advanced techniques and applications, as discussed in the following chapters.

ADVANCED PROMPT CRAFTING TECHNIQUES

After mastering the basics of prompt crafting with ChatGPT, the next step is to explore advanced techniques that can further enhance the effectiveness of your interactions. This chapter delves into sophisticated strategies for prompt crafting, enabling you to extract more nuanced and precise responses from ChatGPT.

One advanced technique is the use of structured prompts. Structured prompts are carefully designed to guide ChatGPT in a specific direction or to elicit a particular type of response. This involves crafting prompts with a clear sequence or format, such as step-by-step instructions, a series of questions, or a detailed scenario description. By providing structure, you help the AI to focus on the key elements of your request, leading to more targeted responses.

Another technique involves leveraging the context window effectively. ChatGPT has a limited amount of text it can consider at any one time (known as the context window). By strategically structuring your prompts and follow-up interactions, you can maximize the use of this context window, ensuring that the most relevant information is always within ChatGPT's immediate scope.

Tailoring prompts to the AI's training data can also yield better results. Understanding the kind of data ChatGPT was trained on can help in formulating prompts that align with its knowledge base.

For instance, prompts that mirror the style or format of text found in typical training datasets may enable ChatGPT to generate more accurate and coherent responses.

Incorporating feedback loops into your prompts is a sophisticated way to refine the AI's responses. This involves providing feedback on ChatGPT's previous responses and asking it to revise or expand upon its answers. Through iterative feedback, you can steer ChatGPT towards a more accurate understanding of your request and a more precise response.

Another advanced strategy is the use of creative phrasing or unconventional prompts. This technique can be particularly useful for generating creative content, solving problems, or exploring topics in novel ways. By phrasing your prompts creatively or presenting unique scenarios, you can encourage ChatGPT to think 'outside the box' and produce more inventive responses.

Finally, understanding and utilizing the latest features and capabilities of ChatGPT is crucial for advanced prompt crafting. Keeping up to date with updates and new developments in ChatGPT's capabilities allows you to take advantage of enhanced functionalities and improved response quality.

By employing these advanced prompt crafting techniques, you can engage with ChatGPT in more sophisticated and effective ways. These strategies open up new possibilities for utilizing the AI tool, from complex problem-solving to creative exploration, and pave the way for more innovative applications, as explored in the upcoming chapters.

ASKING EFFECTIVE QUESTIONS: TIPS AND TRICKS

Mastering the art of asking effective questions is essential for maximizing the potential of ChatGPT. This chapter provides essential tips and strategies to help you formulate questions that lead to clear, relevant, and comprehensive responses from the AI.

A fundamental starting point is to ask clear and direct questions. Ambiguity can lead to vague responses, so specificity is key. Clearly stating what you want to know or learn from ChatGPT helps the AI to understand and address your query accurately.

When your goal is to obtain detailed or exploratory responses, open-ended questions are particularly effective. These questions, which generally can't be answered with a simple 'yes' or 'no,' encourage ChatGPT to provide more in-depth, thoughtful, and comprehensive answers. They are ideal for gaining insights, exploring ideas, or understanding complex topics in greater depth.

In contrast, when you need specific, concise information, closed questions are the way to go. These questions, answerable with a 'yes,' 'no,' or another straightforward response, help focus ChatGPT's answers and are useful for clarifying details or confirming facts.

Phrasing your questions appropriately can significantly impact the quality of responses from ChatGPT. It's often helpful to frame your questions in a way that aligns with how ChatGPT processes information. For example, structuring a question to reflect how similar information might be presented in the AI's training data can lead to more accurate and relevant answers.

The context of your questions also plays a crucial role. Providing ChatGPT with sufficient background information or setting the scene for your query can greatly enhance the relevance and accuracy of its responses. This is particularly important for complex or nuanced topics where the AI needs a clear understanding of the context to respond effectively.

Another strategy is to use follow-up questions to refine or expand upon the responses from ChatGPT. If an initial response isn't quite what you were looking for, a well-crafted follow-up question can help steer the conversation toward the information you need.

Understanding the limitations of ChatGPT is also important. Recognizing that the AI might not always have the latest information or may sometimes misinterpret complex queries can help you adjust your expectations and the way you phrase your questions.

Lastly, experimenting with different styles of questioning and observing how ChatGPT responds is a valuable learning experience. As you become more familiar with the AI's response patterns, you'll be better equipped to ask questions in a way that yields the most useful and accurate information.

By applying these tips and tricks, you'll be well on your way to mastering the skill of asking effective questions, unlocking the full capabilities of ChatGPT. This knowledge will not only enhance your interactions with the AI but also provide a solid foundation for more advanced applications, as explored in subsequent chapters.

INTERPRETING CHATGPT RESPONSES ACCURATELY

Interpreting responses from ChatGPT accurately is crucial for effective communication and realizing the full potential of this AI tool. This chapter is dedicated to guiding you through the nuances of understanding ChatGPT's responses, helping you discern the intended meaning, context, and reliability of the information provided.

The first step in accurate interpretation is recognizing the literal and inferred meanings in ChatGPT's responses. The AI's language model is designed to generate responses based on patterns it has learned from its training data. Therefore, understanding both the explicit content of the response and any implied meanings or contexts is important.

It's also essential to be aware of the limitations of ChatGPT. The AI operates based on the information it was trained on, which means its knowledge is not only finite but also fixed at the point of its last training update. This understanding is critical when interpreting responses, especially for queries about recent events or highly specialized topics.

Evaluating the reliability of the information provided by ChatGPT is another important aspect. While ChatGPT is adept at generating coherent and plausible-sounding responses, it doesn't have the ability to verify the accuracy of its outputs against real-world data.

Cross-referencing information with trusted sources is a recommended practice, particularly for critical or sensitive topics. Contextualizing the responses is key. ChatGPT's replies should be interpreted within the context of the prompt and the conversation. Misinterpretations often occur when responses are taken out of context or when the AI's limitations in understanding nuanced human expressions are overlooked.

Identifying potential biases in responses is also crucial. AI models, including ChatGPT, can inadvertently reflect biases present in their training data. Being mindful of these biases helps in critically assessing the responses and avoiding misinformed conclusions.

Understanding the tone and style of ChatGPT's responses can provide additional insights. ChatGPT can mimic various writing styles and tones, but these are based on the patterns it has learned from its training data. Interpreting the tone correctly can add another layer of understanding to the response.

Finally, engaging in follow-up interactions can clarify ambiguities. If a response from ChatGPT is unclear or incomplete, asking follow-up questions or seeking clarifications can be incredibly helpful. This iterative approach allows you to refine your understanding and obtain more precise information.

By mastering the art of interpreting ChatGPT's responses, you'll be able to engage more effectively with the AI, harnessing its capabilities for a wide range of applications. This skill is not only useful for everyday interactions with ChatGPT but also forms a critical component in more advanced uses of AI, as will be explored in later chapters.

TROUBLESHOOTING COMMON CHATGPT
CHALLENGES

Navigating through the challenges that arise while interacting with ChatGPT is crucial for a seamless experience. This chapter aims to address common issues users may encounter with ChatGPT and offer effective strategies for troubleshooting these problems.

One common challenge is receiving vague or irrelevant responses from ChatGPT. This often occurs when the prompt lacks clarity or specificity. To mitigate this, refine your prompts to be more explicit. Adding context or rephrasing the question can help steer ChatGPT towards a more relevant and accurate response.

Complex queries can sometimes lead to misunderstandings. ChatGPT, despite its advanced capabilities, might struggle with prompts that are multifaceted or require deep understanding of nuanced concepts. In such cases, breaking down your query into simpler, more straightforward components can be beneficial. This allows ChatGPT to process and respond to each part more effectively.

Another issue that may arise is ChatGPT providing outdated or inaccurate information. It's important to remember that ChatGPT's knowledge is based on the data it was trained on, which does not include real-time information.

For queries requiring up-to-date or highly accurate data, it's advisable to cross-reference ChatGPT's responses with current, reliable sources. Users might also face challenges with ChatGPT generating repetitive or generic responses.

This can happen when the AI falls into a pattern based on its training. To counter this, you can modify your prompts by changing the phrasing, asking the question from a different angle, or providing new information that can lead to varied responses.

Sometimes, ChatGPT may produce responses that are too lengthy or detailed for your needs. If you prefer more concise answers, you can instruct ChatGPT explicitly about the desired length or level of detail in your prompt.

Dealing with biases in ChatGPT's responses is another important consideration. AI models can inadvertently reflect biases present in their training data. Being aware of this possibility helps in critically evaluating the responses and using the AI responsibly.

Lastly, technical issues such as connectivity problems, platform errors, or API limitations might hinder your interaction with ChatGPT. These can generally be resolved by checking your internet connection, refreshing the platform, or consulting the technical documentation for any API-related issues.

By understanding and applying these troubleshooting strategies, you can enhance your experience with ChatGPT, making your interactions more efficient and productive. This knowledge is also a stepping stone to more advanced applications of ChatGPT, which will be explored in further chapters.

CREATIVE USES OF CHATGPT

ChatGPT, with its advanced language processing capabilities, offers a playground of creative possibilities. This chapter explores various innovative and imaginative ways in which ChatGPT can be utilized, stretching beyond conventional applications to inspire creativity and foster novel ideas.

One of the most exciting creative uses of ChatGPT is in the realm of writing and storytelling. Whether you are an author struggling with writer's block, a screenwriter looking for dialogue inspirations, or a hobbyist exploring storytelling, ChatGPT can be an invaluable co-creator. By providing a starting point, a plot idea, or character descriptions, ChatGPT can generate narrative pieces, dialogues, and story arcs, offering fresh perspectives and ideas.

In the field of education, ChatGPT can be transformed into a tool for interactive learning. Educators and students can use ChatGPT to create custom learning experiences, such as interactive stories, educational games, or role-playing scenarios. These activities can make learning more engaging and tailored to individual learning styles.

ChatGPT can also be a boon for content creators in digital marketing, blogging, or social media. It can assist in generating creative content ideas, crafting engaging posts, or even writing initial drafts of articles and blogs. While it's important to add a personal touch and ensure accuracy, ChatGPT can significantly streamline the creative process.

For those interested in programming and development, ChatGPT can aid in conceptualizing coding projects or debugging. While it may not write perfect code, it can provide pseudocode, algorithm ideas, or solutions to logical problems, making it a handy companion for brainstorming sessions.

In the arts, ChatGPT can contribute to generating ideas for visual arts, music, or theatre. Artists can use it to explore themes, concepts, or even specific elements like colour schemes or character designs. Musicians and composers can leverage ChatGPT for lyrics writing or to discuss musical concepts.

Additionally, ChatGPT can be used as a tool for language learning and practice. By engaging in conversations, users can practice language skills in a safe and interactive environment. ChatGPT's ability to converse in various languages and dialects makes it a versatile tool for language learners.

Lastly, ChatGPT's potential in creating personalized experiences is vast. From crafting personalized stories and poems to generating custom jokes or recipes, ChatGPT can create unique content tailored to individual preferences or needs.

The creative applications of ChatGPT are limited only by imagination. By leveraging its capabilities, users can explore a vast array of creative pursuits, opening doors to new ideas and innovative applications. This exploration not only enhances the user's experience with ChatGPT but also contributes to the evolving landscape of AI in creativity and beyond.

CHATGPT IN EDUCATION AND LEARNING

The integration of ChatGPT in education and learning heralds a new era of interactive and personalized learning experiences. This chapter delves into the various ways ChatGPT can be utilized to enhance education, offering innovative strategies for students, educators, and lifelong learners.

ChatGPT's role as an educational assistant is one of its most impactful applications. Students can use ChatGPT for help with homework, understanding complex concepts, or getting explanations on various topics. Its ability to provide information in an easily digestible and conversational manner makes it an excellent tool for learning and revision.

Educators can leverage ChatGPT to design engaging curriculum content and interactive learning activities. ChatGPT can assist in creating educational scenarios, problem-solving exercises, or even mock debates, which can be integrated into lesson plans to enhance student engagement and understanding.

ChatGPT also serves as a versatile tool for language learning. Its capacity to converse in multiple languages and at various levels of proficiency makes it an ideal companion for language learners.

From practicing conversational skills to learning vocabulary and grammar, ChatGPT offers a responsive and interactive platform for language acquisition.

In higher education and research, ChatGPT can be a valuable resource for brainstorming research topics, generating hypotheses, or even assisting in literature reviews. While it should not replace rigorous academic research, ChatGPT can provide a starting point and help in exploring various angles of a research topic.

Personalized learning is another significant benefit of ChatGPT in education. It can tailor explanations and content to suit individual learning styles and paces, offering a more customized learning experience. This adaptability makes it especially useful for learners who require additional support or prefer self-paced learning.

ChatGPT can also contribute to developing critical thinking and digital literacy skills. By interacting with an AI tool, learners can practice evaluating information, asking insightful questions, and discerning the reliability of AI-generated content, which are crucial skills in the digital age.

Furthermore, ChatGPT can be a resource for career guidance and professional development. It can provide insights on various career paths, suggest educational resources, and offer advice on skill development, supporting individuals in their professional growth.

The potential of ChatGPT in the educational sphere is vast and multifaceted. By harnessing its capabilities, educators and learners can explore new dimensions of interactive and personalized education. As technology continues to evolve, ChatGPT's role in education is poised to expand, offering exciting opportunities for innovation in teaching and learning methodologies.

PROFESSIONAL APPLICATIONS: CHATGPT IN THE WORKPLACE

The integration of ChatGPT into the professional landscape marks a significant advancement in workplace efficiency and innovation. This chapter explores the diverse applications of ChatGPT in various professional settings, highlighting how this AI tool can streamline processes, enhance productivity, and foster creativity in the workplace.

One of the primary applications of ChatGPT in the professional realm is in communication and customer service. ChatGPT can be employed to manage customer inquiries, provide support, and automate routine communications. Its ability to handle a high volume of requests simultaneously and provide instant responses can significantly improve customer satisfaction and operational efficiency.

In the field of content creation and marketing, ChatGPT serves as a powerful tool for generating ideas, creating draft content, and even assisting with copywriting. Its language capabilities enable it to produce creative and engaging material, from blog posts to marketing copy, which can be refined and personalized by human professionals.

ChatGPT also finds its place in the realm of human resources. It can streamline various HR processes, such as answering employee queries, assisting with onboarding, and even helping with preliminary stages of recruitment by screening candidates or drafting job descriptions.

For project management and planning, ChatGPT can aid in organizing tasks, brainstorming project ideas, and providing suggestions for project optimization. Its ability to process and generate structured information makes it a valuable tool for project managers seeking to optimize workflows and enhance team collaboration.

In the legal and compliance sector, ChatGPT can assist professionals by providing preliminary research, summarizing legal documents, or helping to draft standard contracts. While it does not replace the need for expert legal interpretation, it can serve as a supportive tool to streamline preliminary tasks.

In the technical and IT sectors, ChatGPT can be a helpful resource for coding assistance, debugging, and problem-solving. Programmers and developers can use it to brainstorm coding solutions, understand complex algorithms, or even learn new programming languages.

Furthermore, ChatGPT's role in education and training within the workplace is significant. It can be used to create interactive training modules, simulate scenarios for skill development, and provide personalized learning experiences for employees.

The versatility of ChatGPT in professional settings is considerable. Its ability to adapt to different industries and functions makes it a valuable asset in the modern workplace. By leveraging ChatGPT, businesses and organizations can not only increase efficiency but also foster a culture of innovation and continuous improvement.

As AI technology continues to evolve, ChatGPT's role in the workplace is poised to grow, offering exciting prospects for the future of professional work environments.

INTEGRATING CHATGPT WITH OTHER TOOLS

The integration of ChatGPT with other digital tools and platforms can significantly amplify its utility and impact. This chapter discusses the various ways ChatGPT can be combined with different technologies, enhancing its functionality and extending its applications across various domains.

One of the most potent integrations of ChatGPT is with customer relationship management (CRM) systems. By embedding ChatGPT into a CRM, businesses can automate and personalize customer interactions, improve response times, and gain deeper insights into customer needs and behaviours.

In the realm of software development, ChatGPT can be integrated with coding environments and version control systems. This integration can assist developers in writing code, debugging, and managing documentation, thereby streamlining the development process and enhancing productivity.

ChatGPT can also be merged with business intelligence tools. By integrating ChatGPT with data analytics platforms, companies can generate natural language summaries of complex data, making insights more accessible and understandable for decision-makers.

Integrating ChatGPT with educational platforms and learning management systems (LMS) can revolutionize the way education is delivered. ChatGPT can provide personalized tutoring, answer student queries, and assist in creating interactive and engaging educational content.

In content creation and digital marketing, ChatGPT's integration with content management systems (CMS) and social media platforms can facilitate the generation of creative content, automate responses to audience interactions, and help in crafting marketing strategies.

For project management, incorporating ChatGPT into project management tools can aid in task automation, brainstorming project ideas, and facilitating team communication, thereby enhancing efficiency and collaborative efforts.

The integration of ChatGPT with translation services can create a powerful tool for breaking language barriers in international communication and business. It can assist in real-time translation and localization of content, making global interactions more seamless.

In the healthcare sector, integrating ChatGPT with medical databases and electronic health records (EHR) systems can assist healthcare providers in information retrieval, patient communication, and even preliminary diagnosis, all while ensuring compliance with privacy regulations.

Finally, combining ChatGPT with e-commerce platforms can transform the online shopping experience. It can provide personalized shopping assistance, product recommendations, and customer support, improving the overall customer experience.

The potential of integrating ChatGPT with other tools is vast and continually expanding. These integrations not only enhance the capabilities of ChatGPT but also open up new avenues for innovation and efficiency across various industries. As technology continues to advance, the possibilities for such integrations will only grow, offering exciting prospects for the future of AI in the digital ecosystem.

CHATGPT FOR PROGRAMMING AND DEVELOPMENT

The application of ChatGPT in the field of programming and software development represents a significant leap in the way developers interact with AI to enhance their workflows. This chapter explores how ChatGPT can be utilized by programmers and developers, offering assistance in coding, debugging, and various stages of software development.

One of the keys uses of ChatGPT in programming is as a code assistant. Developers can use ChatGPT to brainstorm ideas for writing code, understand complex algorithms, or seek suggestions for implementing specific functionalities. While ChatGPT does not replace the expertise of seasoned programmers, it can provide valuable insights and alternative approaches to coding problems.

ChatGPT can also be instrumental in the debugging process. By describing the issues, they are facing, developers can use ChatGPT to get suggestions on where the problem might lie and how to resolve it. ChatGPT's ability to process and understand technical language makes it a useful tool for diagnosing and troubleshooting code errors.

Another application of ChatGPT in programming is in learning and skill development. Beginners and experienced programmers alike can use ChatGPT to learn new programming languages, understand complex concepts, or stay updated with the latest programming trends and best practices. ChatGPT's interactive nature makes it an excellent tool for continuous learning and professional growth.

In the realm of documentation and knowledge sharing, ChatGPT can assist in creating documentation for software projects, thereby streamlining one of the more time-consuming aspects of development. It can help generate clear, concise, and user-friendly documentation, making it easier for other developers to understand and use the code.

ChatGPT can also contribute to project planning and brainstorming sessions. It can offer suggestions on project structure, provide insights on potential challenges, and help in formulating solutions, making it a valuable collaborator in the early stages of software development. Moreover, ChatGPT can be integrated into development tools and IDEs (Integrated Development Environments). This integration can provide real-time assistance and feedback to developers, enhancing productivity and efficiency in the coding process.

In the area of testing and quality assurance, ChatGPT can be used to generate test cases or understand the intricacies of different testing methodologies.

Its comprehensive understanding of programming concepts makes it a useful ally in ensuring the robustness and reliability of software. Lastly, ChatGPT can play a role in collaborative development environments. By facilitating communication and helping clarify technical concepts, it can enhance collaboration among team members, especially in distributed teams or when mentoring junior developers.

The utilization of ChatGPT in programming and software development opens up a plethora of opportunities for efficiency and innovation. As AI technology continues to evolve, ChatGPT's role in this field is set to become increasingly significant, offering developers a powerful tool to augment their skills and capabilities.

ETHICAL CONSIDERATIONS IN USING CHATGPT

In the realm of artificial intelligence, the use of technologies like ChatGPT introduces a range of ethical considerations that both developers and users must navigate carefully. This chapter delves into these ethical aspects, highlighting the importance of responsible use and development of AI tools like ChatGPT.

A primary ethical concern is the presence of biases in AI models. ChatGPT, trained on vast and varied data sets, may inadvertently reflect biases present in its training material. These biases could manifest in the AI's responses, potentially leading to unfair or discriminatory outcomes. Users must be aware of this possibility and employ ChatGPT judiciously, especially in sensitive or critical contexts.

Privacy and data security are paramount when interacting with AI tools like ChatGPT. Users should be cautious about sharing personal or sensitive information in their prompts, as this data could be stored or processed in ways that might not align with their privacy expectations. Understanding the data handling and privacy policies of the platform hosting ChatGPT is essential for informed usage.

The issue of misinformation and the accuracy of information provided by ChatGPT is another ethical consideration. While ChatGPT can generate information that is coherent and plausible, it does not have the capability to verify the factual accuracy of its outputs.

Users should cross-reference AI-generated information with reliable sources, especially when dealing with important decisions or topics. The deployment of ChatGPT in various sectors also raises ethical questions around the replacement of human labour.

While ChatGPT can enhance efficiency and productivity, its use should complement human skills rather than replace them. It's important to consider the potential social and economic impacts, ensuring that the adoption of

AI tools like ChatGPT contributes positively to the workforce. Transparency in the use of ChatGPT is also crucial. Users should be aware when they are interacting with an AI system, and the limitations of ChatGPT should be clearly communicated. This transparency is essential for building trust and ensuring that users have realistic expectations of the tool's capabilities.

Finally, the ethical use of ChatGPT extends to the responsibility of AI developers and practitioners. They must ensure that the AI they develop is not only technically sound but also ethically aligned. This involves ongoing efforts to identify and mitigate biases, protect user privacy, and ensure the responsible deployment of the technology.

In conclusion, the ethical considerations surrounding the use of ChatGPT are complex and multifaceted. Both users and developers must engage with these AI tools thoughtfully, considering the broader implications of their use. By prioritizing ethical considerations, we can ensure that technologies like ChatGPT are used in ways that are beneficial, responsible, and aligned with societal values.

UNDERSTANDING AND COUNTERING BIASES IN AI

The issue of bias in artificial intelligence (AI) systems, including ChatGPT, is a critical concern that requires careful attention and action. This chapter addresses the nature of AI biases, their implications, and strategies for understanding and countering these biases to ensure fair and equitable use of AI technologies.

AI systems, including language models like ChatGPT, are trained on large datasets that consist of human-generated content. These datasets can contain biases and stereotypes, which the AI can inadvertently learn and perpetuate. Bias in AI can manifest in various forms, such as gender bias, racial bias, cultural bias, and more, leading to skewed or unfair outcomes.

The first step in countering AI bias is awareness and acknowledgment. Users and developers need to recognize that AI systems can, and often do, exhibit biases. This awareness is crucial for taking proactive steps to mitigate bias in AI applications.

One of the key strategies for countering biases involves diversifying training data. Ensuring that the data used to train AI systems is representative of different demographics, cultures, and perspectives can help reduce the likelihood of biased outcomes. This includes not only diversifying the data sources but also carefully curating the data to eliminate prejudiced or stereotypical content.

In addition to diversifying training data, continuous monitoring and testing for biases in AI responses are essential. Regular audits and assessments can help identify and address any biases that the AI system might exhibit. This requires developing robust methodologies and metrics to measure and evaluate bias.

Engaging diverse teams in AI development and decision-making processes is also vital. A diverse team brings varied perspectives and is more likely to identify potential biases and ethical concerns that might be overlooked otherwise.

Transparency in AI operations and decision-making processes is another crucial factor in countering biases. Users should have clarity on how AI systems, like ChatGPT, generate responses and make decisions. This transparency helps in building trust and facilitates the identification and rectification of biases.

Educating users and developers about the nature and impact of AI biases is equally important. Providing training and resources on ethical AI usage, bias identification, and mitigation strategies can empower individuals to use AI more responsibly.

Finally, fostering an open dialogue and collaboration among stakeholders in the AI ecosystem, including researchers, developers, users, ethicists, and policymakers, is essential for addressing biases in AI. Collective efforts can lead to the development of more equitable and ethical AI systems.

In conclusion, understanding and countering biases in AI is a complex yet essential task. By adopting a multifaceted approach that includes data diversification, continuous monitoring, team diversity, transparency, education, and collaboration, we can work towards minimizing biases and ensuring that AI technologies like ChatGPT are used in a fair and just manner.

PRIVACY AND SECURITY WITH CHATGPT

The advent of AI technologies like ChatGPT brings to the forefront the critical issues of privacy and security. This chapter focuses on the importance of maintaining robust privacy practices and ensuring security while interacting with ChatGPT, outlining strategies to safeguard sensitive information in the age of advanced AI.

When engaging with ChatGPT, understanding the privacy implications is essential. The AI processes inputs to generate responses, and in some cases, this data might be stored or used for model refinement. Users must familiarize themselves with the data handling policies of the hosting platform to ensure informed usage.

Exercising caution in data sharing is pivotal. Users should avoid discussing sensitive personal information or sharing confidential details like identification numbers, financial data, or proprietary business information. This precaution helps in mitigating the risk of data breaches or misuse.

The security measures of the platform offering ChatGPT access are also crucial. Users should assess how the platform secures data transmission, storage, and access. Opting for platforms with strong security protocols enhances protection against unauthorized data exploitation.

Handling the outputs from ChatGPT requires discretion, especially if they contain information based on sensitive inputs. Users should be careful about where and how they share these outputs to prevent unintended exposure of private information.

Compliance with privacy regulations is a shared responsibility. Users, along with service providers, must ensure adherence to laws like the GDPR in the EU or other regional data protection legislations. This adherence is key to legal and ethical data handling.

Awareness and training about privacy and security risks associated with AI tools are indispensable. Users equipped with knowledge of safe AI practices can better navigate the landscape of AI interactions while protecting their personal data.

For developers and businesses leveraging ChatGPT, the responsibility extends to incorporating privacy and security considerations in AI system design and deployment. This approach ensures ethical usage and safeguarding of user data.

Continuous monitoring and updating of security measures are imperative in keeping pace with evolving digital threats. As AI technologies advance, so should the strategies to protect them and the data they handle.

In conclusion, privacy and security in the use of ChatGPT are of paramount importance. A concerted effort from users, developers, and platform providers to uphold strong privacy standards and implement effective security measures is essential. By doing so, the vast potential of AI technologies like ChatGPT can be harnessed without compromising the privacy and security of user information.

BUILDING CUSTOM SOLUTIONS WITH CHATGPT

The versatility of ChatGPT allows for the creation of custom solutions tailored to specific needs and objectives. This chapter explores the potential of ChatGPT in developing personalized applications, offering guidance on how to leverage its capabilities to build innovative and effective solutions.

At the heart of building custom solutions with ChatGPT is understanding its core functionality as a language model. This understanding enables the identification of areas where ChatGPT can be effectively applied, such as automating customer service, creating personalized content, or enhancing data analysis with natural language processing.

The first step in developing a custom solution is defining the specific problem or need. This clarity helps in designing a solution that not only integrates ChatGPT effectively but also aligns with the intended goals. Whether it's improving user engagement, automating repetitive tasks, or providing analytical insights, a well-defined objective is crucial.

Once the problem is identified, the next phase involves designing the interaction flow with ChatGPT. This includes mapping out how users will interact with the solution, how ChatGPT will process inputs, and how it will generate outputs. Designing an effective interaction flow ensures that the solution is user-friendly and efficient.

Integrating ChatGPT with other technologies and platforms is often a key aspect of building custom solutions. This integration can significantly enhance the functionality of ChatGPT, allowing it to interact with databases, other AI models, or software applications. It opens up possibilities for more complex and powerful solutions.

Developing a custom interface or integrating ChatGPT into an existing interface is another important consideration. The interface should be designed with the end-user in mind, ensuring ease of use and accessibility. A well-designed interface can greatly enhance the user experience and the overall effectiveness of the solution.

Testing and refining the solution is a continuous process. Initial deployment should be followed by rigorous testing to identify any issues or areas for improvement. User feedback is invaluable during this phase, as it provides insights into how the solution is being used and how it can be improved.

Maintaining and updating the solution is crucial for its long-term success. As ChatGPT and other integrated technologies evolve, the solution should be updated to leverage new features and capabilities. Regular maintenance ensures that the solution remains effective and relevant.

In conclusion, building custom solutions with ChatGPT offers a pathway to innovation and efficiency. By understanding ChatGPT's capabilities, clearly defining objectives, designing effective interaction flows, integrating with other technologies, and focusing on user experience, personalized and impactful solutions can be developed. These solutions not only harness the power of AI but also address specific needs in a way that traditional software cannot.

THE ART OF CONVERSATION: ENHANCING HUMAN-AI INTERACTION

The interaction between humans and AI, particularly in conversational AI like ChatGPT, is an evolving art that combines technology with the nuances of human communication. This chapter delves into the strategies and techniques to enhance human-AI interaction, ensuring that conversations with ChatGPT are as effective and natural as possible.

At the core of enhancing human-AI interaction is the understanding of ChatGPT's conversational abilities and limitations. ChatGPT is designed to mimic human-like conversation, but it operates within the confines of its programming and training. Acknowledging these limitations helps in setting realistic expectations and in formulating prompts that are well-suited to ChatGPT's capabilities.

Developing effective prompts is key to meaningful interactions with ChatGPT. This involves being clear, concise, and specific in your questions or commands. A well-crafted prompt not only guides ChatGPT in generating relevant responses but also reduces the likelihood of misunderstandings.

Context management is a critical aspect of human-AI conversation. ChatGPT can maintain context over a series of interactions, but its ability to recall previous inputs is not unlimited.

Being mindful of the context window and periodically reinforcing key details can help maintain a coherent and relevant dialogue. The tone and style of interaction also play a significant role. ChatGPT can adapt its responses based on the tone and style of the prompts. Whether you're seeking a formal, informational response or a more casual, conversational tone, adjusting your language and style accordingly can enhance the interaction.

Embracing the iterative nature of conversation with ChatGPT is important. It might take several exchanges to get the desired information or to steer the conversation in the right direction. Patience and iterative refinement of prompts can lead to more successful interactions.

Understanding and leveraging ChatGPT's capabilities for different applications can also enhance human-AI interaction. From casual conversation to providing information, or even creative writing, tailoring your approach based on the intended use can yield better results.

Being aware of ethical considerations, such as the privacy of information shared in conversations and the potential biases in AI responses, is crucial. This awareness ensures responsible and mindful engagement with ChatGPT.

Finally, the human-AI interaction should be seen as a partnership. While ChatGPT can provide valuable assistance and insights, human oversight and judgment are essential. This collaborative approach maximizes the benefits of ChatGPT while ensuring that the AI complements human capabilities.

In conclusion, enhancing human-AI interaction with ChatGPT is an art that involves understanding the AI's capabilities, crafting effective prompts, managing context, and being mindful of ethical considerations. By mastering this art, users can engage in more productive and meaningful conversations with ChatGPT, harnessing the full potential of this advanced conversational AI.

CHATGPT FOR WRITERS AND CONTENT CREATORS

For writers and content creators, ChatGPT emerges as a revolutionary tool, opening up new avenues for creativity and efficiency. This chapter explores how ChatGPT can be utilized by those in the creative industry, aiding in various aspects of writing and content creation.

ChatGPT's ability to generate text based on prompts makes it an invaluable asset for writers facing writer's block. By providing a starting point, a concept, or a few lines, writers can use ChatGPT to generate ideas, continue storylines, or offer new perspectives on their narratives. This can be particularly useful for fiction writers, scriptwriters, and even journalists looking for creative angles on stories.

In the realm of content creation, especially for digital media, ChatGPT serves as a powerful tool for generating initial drafts, headlines, or content ideas. Content creators can leverage ChatGPT to produce a variety of materials, from blog posts and articles to social media posts and marketing copy. While the generated content may require refinement and personalization, ChatGPT significantly reduces the time and effort involved in the content creation process.

For editors and proof-readers, ChatGPT can assist in the editing process by suggesting rewrites, improving sentence structure, or even checking for grammatical consistency.

It acts as an additional tool in the editor's toolkit, helping to enhance the quality of the written content. ChatGPT also finds its use in brainstorming sessions. Writers and content creators can engage with ChatGPT to explore different themes, plot ideas, or character developments. This interaction can spark creativity and lead to the development of unique and engaging content.

In the educational sector, ChatGPT can be a resource for writing essays, reports, and research papers. Students and researchers can use ChatGPT to draft outlines, generate bibliographies, or even get explanations on complex topics. This can aid in the learning process and improve the quality of academic writing.

Additionally, ChatGPT's multilingual capabilities open up possibilities for translation and localization of content. Writers and content creators looking to reach a broader audience can use ChatGPT to translate and adapt their content for different linguistic and cultural contexts.

However, it's important to note the ethical considerations in using ChatGPT for content creation. Ensuring originality, crediting inspiration, and avoiding plagiarism are crucial. Users must be mindful of these aspects to maintain integrity and authenticity in their creative works.

In conclusion, ChatGPT offers a plethora of opportunities for writers and content creators. Its ability to assist in various stages of the writing and content creation process, from ideation to editing, makes it an invaluable asset in the creative industry. By harnessing the capabilities of ChatGPT, writers and content creators can enhance their productivity, unleash their creativity, and achieve new heights in their craft.

USING CHATGPT FOR RESEARCH AND INFORMATION GATHERING

In the realm of research and information gathering, ChatGPT stands out as a valuable tool, offering assistance in data collection, idea generation, and knowledge exploration. This chapter discusses how ChatGPT can be effectively utilized for research purposes, enhancing the efficiency and depth of information gathering processes.

ChatGPT, with its vast database of knowledge and language processing capabilities, can be a quick source for preliminary research. Researchers, students, and professionals can use ChatGPT to get overviews of topics, summaries of complex subjects, or explanations of specific concepts. This can be particularly useful in the early stages of research, where getting a broad understanding of the subject is essential.

For more specific or detailed queries, ChatGPT can assist in identifying key research papers, authors, or resources that are relevant to the topic of interest. While it does not replace in-depth, manual research, ChatGPT can provide starting points and direct users towards valuable sources of information.

ChatGPT can also be used as a brainstorming tool. By discussing ideas or hypotheses with ChatGPT, users can explore various angles of their research topic, uncover new perspectives, or even identify potential gaps in the existing literature. This interactive approach to brainstorming can stimulate creative thinking and lead to more innovative research approaches.

In the synthesis and analysis of research findings, ChatGPT can offer support in organizing and structuring information. It can help in drafting outlines for research papers, reports, or presentations, making the process of compiling and presenting research findings more streamlined.

For researchers dealing with multilingual sources, ChatGPT's ability to understand and generate text in multiple languages can be an asset. It can aid in the initial translation and interpretation of non-English research materials, although users should be mindful of the need for accurate and professional translation for formal research purposes.

Moreover, ChatGPT can be a quick reference for factual verification and fact-checking. While it should not be the sole source of fact-checking, ChatGPT can provide quick answers to factual questions or point to resources where accurate information can be found.

It's important to note the limitations of ChatGPT in research contexts. The information provided by ChatGPT is only as current as its last training data, and it may not include the most recent research developments or publications.

Therefore, it should be used as a supplementary tool rather than a primary source of research information.

In conclusion, ChatGPT offers a range of functionalities that can enhance the research and information-gathering process. Its ability to provide quick overviews, assist in brainstorming, and offer organizational support makes it a valuable tool for researchers, students, and professionals. By understanding and leveraging the capabilities of ChatGPT, users can achieve greater efficiency and depth in their research endeavours.

LANGUAGE LEARNING WITH CHATGPT

The application of ChatGPT in language learning opens up innovative avenues for acquiring and practicing new languages. This chapter explores how ChatGPT can be utilized as a tool for language learners, providing an interactive and flexible platform for language acquisition and practice.

ChatGPT, with its advanced language processing capabilities, is well-suited for assisting in language learning. Its ability to understand and generate text in multiple languages makes it an excellent resource for learners at various proficiency levels. Learners can engage in conversations with ChatGPT in the target language, allowing them to practice and improve their language skills in a safe and controlled environment.

One of the key benefits of using ChatGPT for language learning is its accessibility and flexibility. Learners can interact with ChatGPT at their own pace and on their own schedule, making it a convenient tool for regular practice. Whether it's for short daily practice sessions or more extended interactions, ChatGPT can adapt to the learner's needs.

ChatGPT can assist in expanding vocabulary and improving grammar. Learners can ask ChatGPT to provide definitions, synonyms, and examples of words in context, which can be particularly helpful in building vocabulary.

Additionally, by conversing with ChatGPT, learners can get a better grasp of grammatical structures and usage in the target language. For pronunciation practice, while ChatGPT primarily operates in text format, its responses can be used as a script for pronunciation exercises. Learners can read aloud the responses from ChatGPT and even use voice recognition tools to check their pronunciation.

ChatGPT can also be used to explore cultural nuances and colloquialisms in the target language. Through conversations, learners can ask about cultural references, idiomatic expressions, and slang, helping them understand not just the language but also the cultural context in which it is used.

Moreover, ChatGPT can support learners in practicing real-life conversation scenarios. From ordering food in a restaurant to conducting a business meeting, learners can simulate various scenarios with ChatGPT, gaining confidence and fluency in using the language in different contexts.

It's important to note that while ChatGPT is a valuable tool for language learning, it should be used in conjunction with other learning methods and resources. Language learners should also engage with native speakers, listen to language audio materials, and immerse themselves in the culture of the language for a more comprehensive learning experience.

In conclusion, ChatGPT offers a unique and effective approach to language learning. Its ability to provide interactive, personalized, and context-rich conversations makes it an invaluable tool for learners looking to enhance their language proficiency. By incorporating ChatGPT into their language learning journey, learners can enjoy a more dynamic and engaging experience as they work towards language mastery.

CHATGPT FOR ENTERTAINMENT AND GAMING

In the realms of entertainment and gaming, ChatGPT emerges as a versatile tool, enhancing user experiences with its interactive and creative capabilities. This chapter explores the various ways in which ChatGPT can be integrated into entertainment and gaming, offering new dimensions of engagement and interaction.

In the world of gaming, ChatGPT can be used to create dynamic and responsive narratives. Game developers can leverage ChatGPT to generate dialogues, plot twists, and character interactions, making games more immersive and personalized. In role-playing games (RPGs), for instance, ChatGPT can be used to craft unique storylines and responses based on players' choices, enhancing the depth and replay ability of the game.

ChatGPT also has the potential to serve as an interactive companion or character within games. It can be programmed to respond to player inputs in real-time, adding a layer of interaction that goes beyond pre-scripted game mechanics. This can be particularly engaging in adventure games, simulations, and educational games, where ChatGPT's conversational ability adds to the richness of the gaming experience.

Beyond traditional gaming, ChatGPT can be utilized in interactive storytelling and digital experiences. Writers and creators can use ChatGPT to develop interactive stories, choose-your-own-adventure narratives, and even complex story-based puzzles. This application opens up new forms of digital storytelling, where the user's choices directly influence the direction and outcome of the story.

In the entertainment industry, ChatGPT can assist in content creation for various media, including writing scripts for shows, creating jokes for stand-up comedy, or generating ideas for podcasts. Its ability to understand and generate human-like text makes it a valuable tool for brainstorming and developing initial drafts.

ChatGPT can also enhance interactive experiences in virtual and augmented reality (VR/AR). By integrating ChatGPT into VR/AR environments, developers can create more interactive and responsive virtual worlds. ChatGPT can be used to simulate conversations with virtual characters, provide information or guidance within the VR/AR experience, and even facilitate language learning in an immersive setting.

Furthermore, ChatGPT has applications in social media entertainment. It can be used to generate creative and engaging content for social media platforms, assist in responding to comments or messages, and even help in managing online communities by providing automated moderation or interaction.

It's important to recognize the limitations and ethical considerations in using ChatGPT in entertainment and gaming. Ensuring originality, respecting intellectual property, and maintaining appropriate content are essential. Users and creators should be mindful of these aspects to ensure a positive and respectful entertainment experience.

In conclusion, ChatGPT offers exciting possibilities for innovation in entertainment and gaming. Its ability to generate interactive, personalized, and creative content opens up new avenues for engagement and enjoyment. As technology continues to advance, the potential applications of ChatGPT in these fields are bound to expand, offering unique and captivating experiences to users around the world.

PERSONALIZING YOUR CHATGPT EXPERIENCE

Personalizing the ChatGPT experience is key to maximizing its utility and enhancing user interaction. This chapter discusses various strategies to tailor ChatGPT's responses and functionalities to individual preferences and needs, ensuring a more engaging and relevant experience.

The customization of ChatGPT begins with the user's approach to prompting. Users can refine the style and content of their prompts to align with their specific interests or requirements. For instance, if a user is interested in detailed explanations, they can phrase their prompts to elicit more comprehensive responses. Similarly, for concise information, prompts can be structured to be direct and to the point.

Another aspect of personalization involves teaching ChatGPT about specific topics or preferences. Users can provide background information or context in their prompts, enabling ChatGPT to tailor its responses based on this personalized data. This is particularly useful for niche topics or specialized areas of interest.

Users can also leverage follow-up questions and feedback to shape the conversation's direction and tone. By providing feedback on ChatGPT's responses, users can guide the AI to better align with their conversational preferences, whether that's a formal, informative tone or a more casual, friendly style.

Integrating ChatGPT with personal data sources can further enhance personalization, especially in applications like task management, content recommendation, or personalized learning. However, it's crucial to consider privacy and data security when integrating personal data into AI systems.

Customization can also be achieved by integrating ChatGPT with other tools and platforms that the user frequently uses. For instance, incorporating ChatGPT into a personal project management tool or a learning platform can create a more seamless and customized user experience. Developers and tech-savvy users can take personalization a step further by fine-tuning the ChatGPT model itself or building custom applications using the ChatGPT API. This allows for more advanced customizations tailored to specific use cases or business needs.

For educational or language learning purposes, users can customize their ChatGPT experience to suit their learning goals. This can involve adjusting the complexity of the language used by ChatGPT, focusing on specific topics, or using ChatGPT to simulate particular scenarios or conversations.

Lastly, personalizing the ChatGPT experience is an ongoing process. Users should continually refine their prompts, provide feedback, and explore new ways of interaction to keep the experience aligned with their evolving needs and interests.

In conclusion, personalizing the ChatGPT experience is about leveraging the AI's capabilities in a way that best suits individual preferences, needs, and goals. Through tailored prompts, feedback, integration with personal tools, and even model customization, users can create a unique and fulfilling ChatGPT experience.

As the technology continues to evolve, so too will the opportunities for personalization, offering even more ways for users to engage with ChatGPT in meaningful and productive ways.

THE FUTURE OF AI: BEYOND CHATGPT

Exploring the future of artificial intelligence (AI) extends well beyond the current capabilities of ChatGPT, leading us into a realm of transformative potential and innovation. This chapter delves into the anticipated advancements in AI, potential developments, and the broader implications these may have on various aspects of society.

As we look ahead, language models like ChatGPT are expected to evolve significantly. Future iterations may exhibit enhanced understanding and generation of human language, potentially overcoming current constraints related to context retention, nuance interpretation, and emotional intelligence. Such advancements could lead to more sophisticated, versatile conversational AI systems that mimic human interactions more closely.

The application of AI is poised to expand into increasingly diverse fields. We can anticipate AI playing a pivotal role in areas such as advanced healthcare diagnostics, personalized education, automated creative design, and much more. The integration of AI across various sectors is likely to become more seamless and widespread, enhancing efficiency and fostering new avenues for innovation.

Personalization and interactivity in AI systems are expected to reach new heights. Future AI might offer unprecedented levels of adaptation to individual user preferences, learning styles, and emotional states.

This evolution will significantly alter our interaction with technology, making it more responsive and intuitive to individual needs. A critical aspect of the future of AI will be the emphasis on ethical AI and governance.

As AI becomes more embedded in our daily lives, addressing challenges related to privacy, security, bias, and societal impact will be imperative. Developing comprehensive frameworks and policies to guide the ethical use and governance of AI will be a key focus.

The concept of AI and human collaboration is also likely to gain more prominence. Instead of viewing AI as a replacement for human abilities, there will be a growing emphasis on synergy. AI is expected to augment human skills and creativity, leading to collaborative solutions that combine the best of human and artificial intelligence.

Advancements in AI will also bring challenges, particularly in terms of job displacement and the skills gap. The evolving AI landscape will require a shift in the workforce, with an increasing need for skills that complement AI, such as creativity, critical thinking, and complex problem-solving.

In addition, the democratization of AI is likely to be a significant trend. As AI technologies become more accessible and user-friendly, more individuals and organizations will be able to leverage these tools, leading to widespread adoption and innovation.

In conclusion, the future of AI, extending beyond ChatGPT, holds immense potential for transforming various facets of our world. From revolutionizing industries to redefining our interaction with technology, the trajectory of AI is one of continuous advancement and profound impact. As we navigate this future, a balanced approach that embraces the benefits of AI while addressing its challenges will be crucial for realizing its full potential.

CASE STUDIES: SUCCESSFUL CHATGPT INTERACTIONS

The real-world application of ChatGPT across different sectors provides insightful examples of its capabilities and potential. This chapter showcases various case studies that highlight successful interactions with ChatGPT, illustrating its versatility and impact in practical scenarios.

In the first case study, a high school teacher integrated ChatGPT as a tool for personalized tutoring. The AI was used to simplify complex scientific concepts, assist in solving math problems, and support language learning. This innovative approach led to noticeable improvements in student engagement and comprehension, showcasing ChatGPT's utility as an educational aid.

The second case study focuses on a small business that implemented ChatGPT for customer service automation. By using ChatGPT to handle routine inquiries, the business was able to significantly reduce response times and enhance customer satisfaction. This example highlights the efficiency and effectiveness of ChatGPT in streamlining business processes.

In another instance, a content creator utilized ChatGPT for brainstorming and generating initial drafts for articles and blog posts. ChatGPT's ability to produce creative and coherent content ideas saved the creator considerable time and effort, demonstrating its value in the content creation process.

A notable case study in the healthcare sector involved ChatGPT assisting medical researchers. The AI was used to collate and summarize research papers, enabling researchers to quickly gather pertinent information and insights for their studies. This application underscored ChatGPT's potential in supporting complex research tasks.

In the realm of programming and software development, a case study highlighted ChatGPT's role in assisting developers with coding challenges. ChatGPT provided suggestions for debugging and algorithm development, showcasing its capability as a valuable resource in the software development process.

Another example involved the use of ChatGPT in a legal firm, where it was employed to draft standard legal documents and assist in preliminary legal research. This application demonstrated ChatGPT's versatility and its potential to expedite routine tasks in various professional fields.

In the entertainment industry, a scriptwriter used ChatGPT to explore different dialogue options and character developments for a screenplay. ChatGPT's contributions enriched the creative process, offering new perspectives and ideas.

Each of these case studies demonstrates the diverse applications and benefits of ChatGPT. From enhancing educational experiences to streamlining business operations, aiding in creative processes, and supporting professional tasks, ChatGPT proves to be a versatile and impactful tool. These real-world examples not only illustrate the practical uses of ChatGPT but also inspire new ways to leverage AI technology across various sectors.

MISTAKES TO AVOID WHEN USING CHATGPT

Utilizing ChatGPT effectively requires an understanding of its capabilities and limitations. This chapter highlights common mistakes users make when interacting with ChatGPT, offering insights on how to avoid them and ensure a more productive experience with this advanced AI tool.

A frequent mistake is overestimating ChatGPT's capabilities. While ChatGPT is a sophisticated AI, it is not infallible and has limitations, particularly in understanding highly complex, nuanced, or specialized topics. Users should maintain realistic expectations about the AI's capabilities, recognizing that it is a tool designed to assist rather than replace human expertise.

Another common error is failing to provide clear and specific prompts. Vague or ambiguous prompts often lead to responses that are not targeted or relevant. To get the most out of ChatGPT, users should formulate their prompts with clarity and specificity, guiding the AI to generate more precise and useful responses.

Underestimating the impact of context is also a mistake. ChatGPT's responses are influenced by the context provided in the conversation. Not maintaining a clear thread of context or providing insufficient background information can lead to misunderstandings or less accurate responses from the AI.

Relying solely on ChatGPT for critical decision-making or as a single source of truth can be problematic. While ChatGPT can provide valuable insights and information, it should not be the sole basis for important decisions, especially in professional or high-stakes scenarios. Users should cross-reference ChatGPT's responses with other reliable sources.

Ignoring the ethical implications of using ChatGPT is another oversight. This includes the potential for perpetuating biases present in the AI's training data and the misuse of the tool for deceptive or harmful purposes. Users should be mindful of the ethical considerations and use ChatGPT responsibly.

Not customizing the ChatGPT experience to individual needs can limit its effectiveness. Users have the opportunity to tailor their interactions with ChatGPT based on their specific requirements and preferences. Overlooking this customization can result in a less optimal user experience.

Lastly, disregarding the need for continual learning and adaptation when using ChatGPT is a mistake. As AI technology evolves, so do its functionalities and capabilities. Staying informed about updates and continuously adapting one's approach to using ChatGPT is crucial for maximizing its benefits.

In conclusion, avoiding these common mistakes can significantly enhance the user experience with ChatGPT. By understanding and respecting the tool's capabilities and limitations, formulating clear prompts, maintaining context, and using ChatGPT ethically and responsibly, users can leverage this powerful AI to its full potential.

COMMUNITY AND SUPPORT FOR CHATGPT USERS

The presence of a robust community and support system is crucial for users of advanced technologies like ChatGPT. This chapter explores the various forms of community and support available to ChatGPT users, emphasizing how these resources can enhance the user experience, foster learning, and encourage collaboration.

The ChatGPT user community is diverse, encompassing experts, enthusiasts, developers, and casual users. Engaging with this community can provide valuable insights, tips, and advice on how to effectively use ChatGPT. Online forums, social media groups, and dedicated platforms are common spaces where users can connect, share experiences, and learn from each other.

Online forums and discussion boards are particularly useful for new users and those encountering specific challenges with ChatGPT. These platforms often feature FAQs, troubleshooting guides, and user-generated content that can help in resolving issues and improving usage techniques. Experienced users and developers frequently contribute to these forums, offering their expertise and support to others in the community.

Social media platforms also play a significant role in the ChatGPT user community. They offer a more dynamic and real-time interaction among users.

Social media groups and pages dedicated to ChatGPT provide a space for sharing updates, creative uses of the tool, and discussing the latest advancements in AI. They also facilitate networking and collaboration among users with similar interests.

Official support channels provided by the developers of ChatGPT are another critical resource. These may include help desks, customer support lines, and official documentation. Accessing these resources can be beneficial for technical support, understanding new features, and getting official updates on the tool.

Webinars, workshops, and online courses are excellent resources for structured learning and deeper understanding of ChatGPT. These educational resources often cover a range of topics from basic usage to advanced techniques and can be beneficial for users looking to enhance their skills and knowledge.

Meetups and conferences, either virtual or in-person, provide opportunities for users to interact directly with experts, developers, and other enthusiasts. These events can be a platform for learning about cutting-edge developments in AI, networking, and discovering new applications and tools related to ChatGPT.

User-generated content, such as blogs, tutorials, and video guides, is an invaluable part of the community support for ChatGPT. Experienced users often create and share content that can assist others in navigating and maximizing the potential of ChatGPT.

In conclusion, the community and support ecosystem for ChatGPT users is a rich and diverse network, offering a range of resources for learning, problem-solving, and collaboration. By engaging with these resources, users can enhance their experience with ChatGPT, stay updated on the latest trends, and become part of an evolving and dynamic field.

CHATGPT FOR BUSINESS AND CUSTOMER SERVICE

Incorporating ChatGPT into business operations and customer service can significantly enhance efficiency and customer engagement. This chapter explores the various ways in which businesses can leverage ChatGPT to improve their services, streamline processes, and provide enriched customer experiences.

ChatGPT can be a game-changer in customer service. By integrating ChatGPT into customer support systems, businesses can provide instant, 24/7 responses to customer inquiries. This AI-driven approach can handle a high volume of queries simultaneously, reducing wait times and improving overall customer satisfaction.

The application of ChatGPT in automating routine customer interactions is another significant benefit. It can manage common customer service tasks, such as answering FAQs, providing product information, or guiding customers through basic troubleshooting processes. This frees up human customer service representatives to focus on more complex and nuanced customer issues.

ChatGPT can also be used for personalized customer interactions. By analysing customer data and previous interactions, ChatGPT can offer customized recommendations, advice, or assistance, making each customer's experience more tailored and personal.

In sales and marketing, ChatGPT can assist in generating leads, qualifying prospects, and even conducting initial outreach. Its ability to interact in natural language enables it to engage potential customers in a conversational manner, improving the chances of conversion.

Businesses can also use ChatGPT for internal purposes, such as employee training and internal support. ChatGPT can be programmed to provide training modules, answer employee queries about company policies or procedures, and assist in onboarding new staff.

The integration of ChatGPT into business analytics is another area of potential. ChatGPT can help in analysing customer feedback, market trends, or business data, providing insights that can inform business strategies and decision-making.

In e-commerce, ChatGPT can enhance the online shopping experience. It can be used as a virtual shopping assistant, providing product recommendations, assisting with order placement, or answering queries about shipping and returns.

It's important for businesses to be mindful of the limitations and ethical considerations when using ChatGPT. Ensuring accurate and responsible use, respecting customer privacy, and maintaining human oversight are crucial to effectively integrating ChatGPT into business and customer service operations.

In conclusion, ChatGPT offers a range of applications that can transform business operations and customer service. Its ability to automate routine tasks, personalize interactions, and provide valuable insights can help businesses improve efficiency, enhance customer experiences, and stay competitive in a rapidly evolving market.

LEGAL IMPLICATIONS OF AI CONVERSATIONS

The increasing use of AI technologies like ChatGPT in various domains brings to light several legal implications that warrant attention. This chapter addresses key legal aspects associated with AI conversations, including liability, privacy, intellectual property, and regulatory compliance.

Liability issues in AI interactions are complex and multifaceted. When AI systems like ChatGPT offer advice or information leading to detrimental outcomes, it raises questions about who is responsible. The legal quandary often revolves around whether liability rests with the AI developers, the platform providers, the users, or a combination of these entities. As AI technology advances, legal frameworks will need to evolve to address these challenges appropriately.

Privacy and data protection are paramount in the realm of AI conversations. AI models like ChatGPT process and generate vast amounts of data, which may include personal and sensitive information.

Ensuring compliance with data protection laws, such as the General Data Protection Regulation (GDPR) in Europe and other similar regulations worldwide, is critical. Developers and businesses employing AI tools must ensure robust data protection measures are in place to safeguard user privacy.

Intellectual property (IP) concerns are also significant in the context of AI conversations. Issues arise regarding the ownership of content generated by AI, especially when it derives from or mimics copyrighted material. The blurring lines between AI-generated content and human-created content pose challenges in defining and enforcing IP rights. This area of law is still developing, with ongoing debate and legal discourse.

Compliance with regulatory frameworks is another legal aspect that must be considered. This includes adhering to industry-specific regulations that may apply to the use of AI in fields like healthcare, finance, or legal services. Businesses and developers must stay informed about relevant regulations and ensure their AI applications comply with these standards.

Ethical considerations, although not always strictly legal, also play a crucial role in the deployment of AI technologies. This encompasses issues like fairness, bias, transparency, and accountability. While not always codified into law, these ethical principles are increasingly influencing legal and regulatory discussions around AI.

In conclusion, the legal implications of AI conversations are a critical area that requires ongoing attention and adaptation. As AI technologies become more embedded in our daily lives and business operations, legal frameworks will need to keep pace, addressing the unique challenges posed by AI in a way that protects individual rights and promotes responsible innovation.

This chapter underscores the importance of legal diligence for anyone involved in developing, deploying, or using AI technologies like ChatGPT.

CULTURAL IMPACTS OF CHATGPT AND AI

The advent of AI technologies like ChatGPT has far-reaching cultural implications, influencing diverse aspects of society, from communication patterns to educational paradigms and ethical considerations. This chapter delves into these impacts, exploring how ChatGPT and similar AI systems are reshaping cultural norms and human interactions.

The way we communicate has been significantly altered by ChatGPT. The efficiency and convenience of interacting with AI have begun to transform both personal and professional communication spheres. For instance, AI-driven chatbots are increasingly handling customer service interactions, while personal use of AI for information retrieval and casual conversation is becoming more common. These shifts raise questions about the future of human interaction and the role of AI in our daily communications.

In the field of education, ChatGPT has introduced new modalities of learning and information access. Its ability to provide instant, customized responses has made it a valuable tool for students and educators, supplementing traditional teaching methods. However, this also brings challenges, such as ensuring the quality of AI-provided information and maintaining academic integrity.

The influence of ChatGPT on work and employment is another cultural aspect. AI's ability to automate certain tasks has led to changes in job roles and skill requirements. While AI can increase efficiency and create new opportunities, it also poses challenges in terms of job displacement and the need for workforce retraining.

Ethical considerations surrounding AI use are becoming a significant part of the cultural discourse. Issues like privacy, data security, bias in AI algorithms, and the ethical use of AI-generated content are increasingly at the forefront of public and academic discussions. These conversations are shaping how society views and interacts with AI technologies.

The artistic and creative realms are also being reshaped by AI. ChatGPT and similar technologies have been used to create poetry, write scripts, and generate art, challenging traditional notions of creativity and artistic authorship.

Social and cultural biases present in AI, due to their training on historical data, raise important questions about reinforcing societal stereotypes. This has led to a greater emphasis on developing AI that is ethical, unbiased, and culturally sensitive.

In conclusion, the cultural impacts of ChatGPT and AI are profound and multifaceted. These technologies are not only changing the way we communicate, learn, and work but are also influencing broader societal norms and ethical frameworks. As AI continues to evolve, its cultural implications will likely deepen, necessitating ongoing dialogue and thoughtful engagement with these transformative technologies.

STAYING UPDATED: FOLLOWING AI TRENDS

Keeping up-to-date with the rapidly evolving field of artificial intelligence (AI) is essential for anyone interested in or working with technologies like ChatGPT. This chapter outlines various methods and resources to stay informed about the latest trends, developments, and advancements in AI.

Regularly reading industry publications and academic journals is crucial for staying informed. These sources often provide in-depth insights into the latest AI developments, research breakthroughs, and expert opinions. Keeping tabs on reputable AI and technology news outlets, as well as subscribing to relevant academic journals, can help you stay at the forefront of the field.

Online courses, webinars, and workshops offer valuable learning opportunities for those looking to keep up with AI advancements. Many educational platforms and universities offer a range of courses, from introductory to advanced levels, which cater to both newcomers and seasoned professionals in the AI space.

Attending conferences, seminars, and tech meetups is another effective way to stay updated. These events not only provide information on the latest trends and developments but also offer networking opportunities with other AI professionals, researchers, and enthusiasts.

They can be a source of inspiration and a way to gauge the future direction of AI technology. Participating in online forums and AI communities can also be beneficial.

These platforms allow for the exchange of ideas, solutions to common challenges, and discussions on recent advancements in AI. Engaging with these communities can provide practical insights and foster collaborative learning.

Following key influencers, thought leaders, and organizations in the AI field on social media platforms like LinkedIn, Twitter, and YouTube can keep you informed about current discussions, opinions, and news in the AI community.

Experimenting with AI tools and technologies is equally important. Hands-on experience with AI applications, including ChatGPT, allows for a deeper understanding of their capabilities, limitations, and potential use cases. This practical approach can provide a unique perspective on the applicability and impact of AI in various domains.

Staying informed about regulatory changes and ethical considerations in AI is also crucial. As AI becomes more integrated into society, understanding the legal, ethical, and societal implications of AI technologies is vital for responsible usage and development.

In conclusion, staying updated with AI trends requires a combination of continuous learning, active engagement with the AI community, and practical experimentation with AI tools. By utilizing these methods, individuals and organizations can stay informed and adapt to the rapidly changing landscape of AI technology.

EXPLORING GLOBAL AI DEVELOPMENTS

The landscape of artificial intelligence (AI) is not confined to a single region or country; it's a global phenomenon with diverse contributions and impacts across the world. This chapter provides an overview of AI developments on a global scale, examining the unique contributions, collaborations, and challenges presented by different regions and cultures.

AI advancements are occurring at varying paces and in different capacities around the world. In North America, particularly the United States, there's a strong focus on AI research and development, hosting numerous pioneering AI companies and research institutions. Europe, meanwhile, contributes significantly to the discourse on AI governance and ethical standards, with a particular emphasis on privacy and data protection.

Asia is a notable player in the AI domain, with countries like China, South Korea, and Japan making significant strides. China's rapid growth in AI technologies, supported by substantial investments and government backing, positions it as a key influencer in the field. South Korea and Japan are renowned for their advancements in robotics and automation technologies.

International collaborations and partnerships are pivotal in shaping the global AI narrative. These cross-border alliances between academia, industry, and governments facilitate the sharing of knowledge, resources, and innovations. They are instrumental in addressing universal challenges and in driving AI research and application forward.

Emerging economies are increasingly impacted by AI developments. While AI presents opportunities for economic growth and technological advancement in these regions, it also poses challenges, such as addressing the digital divide and managing workforce transitions due to automation.

Cultural and ethical considerations play a significant role in AI's global expansion. Diverse cultural contexts influence the development and deployment of AI technologies. It's crucial to recognize and respect these differences to ensure AI applications are culturally sensitive and ethically sound.

The regulatory landscape for AI varies significantly across the globe. While some regions emphasize innovation and growth, others focus on regulating privacy, security, and ethical implications. Navigating these varied regulatory environments is essential for multinational AI initiatives and collaborations.

However, global AI developments are not without challenges. Issues like data privacy, AI biases, and equitable access to AI technologies are universal concerns that require coordinated efforts to address.

Conversely, the global AI movement presents numerous opportunities, from leveraging AI for societal benefits to enhancing international cooperation and fostering innovation that respects cultural diversity and ethical principles.

In summary, the global developments in AI highlight the diverse, dynamic nature of this field. Understanding these international perspectives is crucial for anyone engaged in AI, offering a comprehensive view of how AI is shaping and being shaped by different regions and societies. This global viewpoint is essential to harness the full potential of AI in a manner that is inclusive, respectful, and beneficial on a worldwide scale.

CHATGPT AND ACCESSIBILITY

Ensuring accessibility in technology is vital, and AI systems like ChatGPT have a significant role to play in this regard. This chapter explores the intersection of ChatGPT with accessibility, examining how this technology can be leveraged to support individuals with disabilities and enhance overall accessibility in digital spaces.

ChatGPT, with its advanced natural language processing capabilities, presents unique opportunities to assist users with various disabilities. For those with visual impairments, ChatGPT can serve as a conversational interface, allowing users to access information and services through voice commands and audio responses. This interaction model can make digital content more accessible, breaking down barriers that traditional text-based interfaces might present.

In the context of hearing impairments, ChatGPT can be used to develop real-time captioning and transcription services. Its ability to quickly process and generate text can provide instant transcriptions of spoken words, facilitating communication for individuals who are deaf or hard of hearing, particularly in educational and professional settings.

For individuals with mobility or dexterity challenges, ChatGPT can reduce the need for physical interaction with devices. Voice-controlled interfaces powered by ChatGPT can enable users to perform various tasks, from browsing the internet to controlling smart home devices, without the need for extensive physical movement.

ChatGPT can also be a valuable tool for people with cognitive disabilities. By offering clear, concise, and easy-to-understand responses, ChatGPT can aid in comprehension and learning, providing information in a format that is more digestible for users with cognitive challenges.

Beyond assisting individuals with specific disabilities, ChatGPT's capabilities can enhance the overall user experience and accessibility of digital platforms. Its ability to understand and respond to natural language queries makes digital content more approachable and user-friendly for a broader audience, including those who might struggle with complex interfaces or technical jargon.

However, the use of ChatGPT in accessibility also presents challenges. Ensuring that AI systems like ChatGPT are designed with accessibility in mind is crucial. This involves considering diverse user needs from the outset and incorporating accessibility features and considerations into the development process.

Additionally, there is a need for ongoing testing and refinement of these systems to ensure they meet the needs of users with disabilities. User feedback and engagement with the disability community are essential in this process, helping developers identify and address any gaps or issues in accessibility.

In conclusion, ChatGPT has the potential to significantly enhance accessibility in the digital world. By providing alternative modes of interaction and understanding, ChatGPT can help make digital content and services more accessible to individuals with disabilities. As the technology continues to evolve, it is imperative that accessibility remains a key consideration, ensuring that AI tools like ChatGPT are inclusive and beneficial for all users.

CHATGPT IN HEALTHCARE AND WELLNESS

Incorporating ChatGPT into healthcare and wellness sectors presents an innovative approach to enhancing patient care, medical research, and health education. This chapter examines the diverse applications of ChatGPT in healthcare, exploring its potential benefits and the challenges that need to be navigated.

ChatGPT can significantly enhance patient interaction and support. It can provide general health information, respond to common medical queries, and offer wellness advice, thereby augmenting the patient care process. For routine inquiries, ChatGPT can offer immediate assistance, reducing the workload on medical professionals and enhancing patient engagement.

In mental health and therapy, ChatGPT can serve as a supplementary tool. It can assist in providing cognitive-behavioural therapy techniques, mindfulness exercises, and supportive conversations. While it cannot replace professional mental health care, ChatGPT can offer additional support and accessible resources for those seeking mental wellness.

The role of ChatGPT in medical education and training is also noteworthy. Medical students and professionals can use ChatGPT as a learning tool to access medical knowledge, study case scenarios, and even practice diagnostic skills through interactive AI conversations.

This application can enrich the learning experience and serve as a valuable supplement to traditional medical education. In terms of health administration, ChatGPT can streamline various administrative tasks such as appointment scheduling, patient data management, and answering routine healthcare queries. This efficiency can lead to improved healthcare delivery and patient satisfaction.

ChatGPT has potential applications in medical research as well. Researchers can utilize ChatGPT for literature reviews, data analysis, and hypothesis generation. Its ability to process vast amounts of information can aid in identifying research gaps and generating new insights in various medical fields.

In public health, ChatGPT can be instrumental in disseminating health information and raising awareness about health conditions and preventive measures. Its scalability makes it a valuable tool for reaching broad audiences with essential health messages.

However, the use of ChatGPT in healthcare comes with challenges. Ensuring accuracy is paramount, as misinformation can have serious consequences in a medical context. Additionally, privacy and confidentiality are critical concerns, especially when handling sensitive patient information. Adhering to healthcare regulations and ethical standards is essential in the deployment of ChatGPT in healthcare settings.

In conclusion, ChatGPT's integration into healthcare and wellness offers promising benefits, including enhanced patient support, improved healthcare administration, and valuable tools for medical education and research. As the technology continues to evolve, it is vital to address the challenges and ensure that its use in healthcare is reliable, secure, and aligned with ethical and regulatory standards.

SUSTAINABLE PRACTICES IN AI

The advancement of artificial intelligence (AI) brings with it a responsibility to adopt sustainable practices. This chapter explores the essential aspects of sustainability in AI, including environmental, ethical, social, and economic factors, crucial for responsible AI development and deployment.

Environmental Impact of AI

A significant concern in sustainable AI practices is the environmental impact, particularly related to energy consumption and carbon footprint. Large AI models like ChatGPT require substantial computational power, leading to high energy use. To mitigate this, there's a growing emphasis on developing energy-efficient AI algorithms, improving the efficiency of data centres, and utilizing renewable energy sources. Such measures are vital to reduce the environmental footprint of AI technologies.

Ethical AI Development

Ethical considerations form the cornerstone of sustainable AI. This involves ensuring AI systems are transparent, fair, and unbiased. It's important to recognize and address potential biases in AI models and strive for algorithms that are equitable and non-discriminatory.

Involving diverse groups in AI development can help reflect a wide range of perspectives, promoting fairness and inclusivity.

Social Sustainability in AI

AI's impact on society is profound, necessitating a focus on social sustainability. This includes developing AI in a way that benefits society, addresses social challenges, and improves quality of life. AI should be accessible to diverse populations, ensuring that its benefits are not limited to specific groups. Additionally, AI applications should respect and preserve cultural and societal norms and values.

Economic Aspects of Sustainable AI

Economic sustainability involves developing AI technologies that contribute positively to the economy, enhance productivity, and create new opportunities while minimizing job displacement. The goal is to leverage AI for economic growth that is inclusive and sustainable, avoiding widening economic disparities.

Sustainable AI Governance

Effective governance structures are essential for sustainable AI. This includes policies and regulations that guide the ethical development, deployment, and use of AI.

Governance frameworks should encourage innovation while safeguarding against risks associated with AI, such as privacy breaches, security issues, and misuse of technology.

Promoting AI Literacy

Increasing AI literacy and awareness is also a key component of sustainable AI practices. Educating the public about AI, its potential benefits, and its limitations can foster more informed and responsible use of AI technologies. This also includes training the workforce with the skills necessary to thrive in an AI-integrated economy.

Research and Collaboration

Sustainable AI requires ongoing research and collaboration among various stakeholders, including technologists, policymakers, academia, and industry leaders. Collaborative efforts can drive forward innovations in AI that are environmentally friendly, socially responsible, and economically viable.

In conclusion, adopting sustainable practices in AI is essential to ensure that the development and application of these technologies are beneficial, ethical, and harmonious with environmental, social, and economic goals. As AI continues to evolve, a commitment to sustainability will be crucial for realizing its full potential in a responsible and beneficial manner.

AI ETHICS: GLOBAL PERSPECTIVES

Understanding the ethical implications of artificial intelligence (AI) requires a global perspective, as cultural, legal, and societal contexts significantly influence how AI ethics are interpreted and implemented. This chapter explores the varied viewpoints and approaches to AI ethics around the world, underscoring the importance of a diverse and inclusive understanding of these issues.

Cultural Influences on AI Ethics

Different cultures bring unique perspectives to the ethics of AI. In Western countries, there is often a strong emphasis on individual privacy and data protection, as reflected in regulations like the GDPR in Europe. This contrasts with some Asian countries, where societal harmony and collective benefits may be prioritized, influencing the development and deployment of AI technologies.

Diverse Legal Frameworks

The legal frameworks governing AI vary significantly across the globe. These differences impact how AI is developed, used, and regulated. For instance, the European Union's approach to AI regulation focuses heavily on human rights and ethical standards, while the United States tends to have a more market-driven approach. Understanding these diverse legal landscapes is crucial for global AI initiatives.

Ethical Principles in AI

While there is no universal consensus on AI ethics, certain key principles are widely recognized, including fairness, transparency, accountability, and non-maleficence. However, the interpretation and prioritization of these principles can vary. For instance, what is considered fair in one culture might be viewed differently in another.

Global Collaboration and Dialogue

Addressing the ethical challenges of AI requires global collaboration and dialogue. International forums and organizations play a vital role in bringing together diverse stakeholders to discuss and formulate ethical guidelines for AI. This collaboration is essential to develop a more harmonious global approach to AI ethics.

Impact of AI on Society

Different societies may experience the impacts of AI in varying ways. Issues such as job displacement, privacy concerns, and the digital divide can have different implications in different regions. It's important to consider these varied societal impacts when discussing the ethics of AI.

Inclusivity and Representation in AI Development

Inclusivity in AI development is critical to ensure that AI systems are not biased and are representative of diverse populations. This includes not only the datasets used for training AI but also the diversity of the teams developing AI technologies.

Future Trends in AI Ethics

Looking ahead, the field of AI ethics is likely to evolve as AI technologies advance and become more integrated into society. Keeping abreast of these changes and continuously engaging in ethical discussions will be essential for the responsible development and use of AI.

In conclusion, AI ethics is a multi-faceted issue that requires a global perspective. Understanding the cultural, legal, and societal contexts in which AI operates is crucial for navigating the ethical challenges it presents. As AI continues to advance, fostering an inclusive and collaborative approach to AI ethics will be key to harnessing its benefits while mitigating its risks.

FUTURE-PROOFING SKILLS IN AN AI WORLD

In an era where artificial intelligence (AI) is reshaping the landscape of work and technology, future-proofing skills becomes crucial. This chapter discusses the types of skills that are likely to remain valuable and in demand in an AI-driven world, and how individuals can develop these skills to stay relevant and competitive.

Emphasizing Soft Skills

While AI excels in technical and data-driven tasks, human soft skills remain irreplaceable. Skills such as critical thinking, creativity, problem-solving, empathy, and emotional intelligence are crucial. These skills enable individuals to interpret data meaningfully, innovate, make ethical decisions, and connect with others on a human level – capabilities that AI cannot replicate.

Technical and Digital Literacy

Technical and digital literacy are becoming foundational skills. Understanding the basics of AI, machine learning, and data analytics is beneficial, regardless of one's field. This doesn't mean everyone needs to be an AI expert but having a fundamental grasp of how these technologies work and their implications is valuable.

Adaptability and Lifelong Learning

The ability to adapt and commit to lifelong learning is perhaps the most crucial skill in an AI world. With the rapid pace of technological change, the willingness to continuously learn, unlearn, and relearn is essential. This includes staying updated with the latest technological trends and being open to new ways of working.

Interdisciplinary Knowledge

Interdisciplinary knowledge and the ability to work across different domains are increasingly important. AI's impact is vast and touches various fields. Professionals who can bridge the gap between AI technology and other disciplines (like healthcare, finance, arts, etc.) are likely to be highly valued.

Collaboration and Teamwork

The future workplace will likely consist of both humans and AI systems working in tandem. Skills in collaboration and teamwork, including the ability to work effectively with AI and automated systems, will be essential. Understanding how to harness the strengths of both human and AI colleagues can lead to more effective and efficient outcomes.

Ethical Judgment and Decision-Making

As AI systems become more prevalent, ethical judgment and decision-making become more significant. Professionals need to navigate the ethical implications of AI and make decisions that consider societal values and norms.

Cultural Competency

The global reach of AI technologies necessitates cultural competency. Understanding and respecting diverse perspectives and customs is important, especially when AI systems are used across different cultural and geographical boundaries.

In conclusion, future-proofing skills in an AI world involves a combination of developing soft skills, technical literacy, adaptability, interdisciplinary knowledge, teamwork, ethical judgment, and cultural competency. By cultivating these skills, individuals can prepare themselves to navigate an AI-integrated future successfully and make the most of the opportunities that AI technologies present.

AI IN ART AND DESIGN

The infusion of artificial intelligence (AI) into the realms of art and design is revolutionizing these fields, offering new tools and possibilities for creativity. This chapter explores the impact of AI on art and design, examining how AI technologies like ChatGPT are being used to inspire, create, and transform artistic and design processes.

AI-Generated Art

AI algorithms, particularly those based on generative models, have the capability to produce unique artworks. These AI-generated pieces can range from visual art, like paintings and digital illustrations, to music compositions and literary works. Artists are using AI as a collaborative tool to push the boundaries of creativity, generating art that blends human imagination with algorithmic complexity.

Design Innovation

In the world of design, AI is being harnessed to automate and optimize various processes. From graphic design to architectural planning, AI tools can analyse vast amounts of data to suggest design modifications, predict trends, and even generate complete design prototypes. This integration of AI in design workflows is enabling designers to explore new concepts and efficiencies.

Personalization in Art and Design

AI technologies enable a high degree of personalization in art and design. By analysing user preferences and inputs, AI can create customized artworks and designs tailored to individual tastes. This personalization is revolutionizing areas such as fashion design, interior decoration, and user interface design, where bespoke and user-centric designs are increasingly in demand.

Interactive Art Experiences

AI is facilitating new forms of interactive art, where the audience becomes a part of the creation process. Interactive installations and performances powered by AI respond to viewer inputs in real-time, creating immersive and dynamic art experiences. This interactivity is blurring the lines between artist, artwork, and audience, redefining the art experience.

Challenges and Ethical Considerations

The use of AI in art and design also presents challenges and ethical considerations. Questions around the originality of AI-generated art, the role of the artist, and copyright issues are being debated. Furthermore, the potential for AI to replicate and perpetuate cultural biases in art and design is a concern that needs to be addressed.

Education and Skill Development

As AI becomes more prevalent in art and design, education and skill development in these fields are evolving. Artists and designers are seeking to learn about AI technologies and how to integrate them into their work. Educational institutions are beginning to incorporate AI into art and design curricula, preparing students for a future where these skills will be increasingly important.

In conclusion, AI's role in art and design is both transformative and expansive. It offers artists and designers new tools for expression and innovation, while also presenting unique challenges and ethical questions. As AI continues to evolve, its influence on art and design is likely to grow, continually reshaping these creative fields.

CONCLUSION: EMBRACING AI FOR A BETTER FUTURE

The exploration of artificial intelligence (AI), particularly through the lens of ChatGPT, has revealed AI as more than a technological marvel; it's a transformative force reshaping diverse facets of our lives and society. This final chapter synthesizes our journey through AI's vast capabilities, applications, and implications, underscoring the significance of embracing AI to unlock its potential for a better future.

AI stands as a catalyst for remarkable change. It has demonstrated its capacity to enhance productivity and spur creativity across various sectors, from business and the arts to healthcare and education. AI's potential to address complex challenges, drive innovation, and open new avenues for growth is immense and largely untapped.

However, embracing AI for a brighter future requires a balanced approach, weighing its potential against the need for responsible stewardship. Addressing ethical, social, and economic challenges is paramount. This includes ensuring AI systems are fair and equitable, safeguarding privacy and security, and preparing for the transformative impact AI will have on the workforce and employment landscape.

Sustainable development of AI calls for collaborative efforts spanning different sectors. Governments, businesses, academia, and civil society need to join forces to establish policies and frameworks that guide responsible AI development and usage.

Such collaboration is vital for maximizing the benefits of AI while minimizing potential risks and adverse impacts. As AI becomes increasingly integrated into daily life, fostering AI literacy and education becomes crucial.

Equipping individuals with the knowledge and skills to effectively interact with AI, comprehend its broader implications, and utilize it to its full potential is essential. This education will empower people to navigate an AI-augmented world confidently.

The future of AI is laden with both opportunities and challenges. The rapid evolution of AI promises new innovations and applications, continually reshaping our interaction with technology. Navigating this future will require adaptability, a commitment to continuous learning, and a willingness to embrace the transformative nature of AI.

In conclusion, embracing AI for a better future entail recognizing its transformative capabilities while being acutely aware of its complexities and challenges. The journey ahead with AI offers opportunities to enhance human experience, work, and societal functioning.

By adopting a balanced perspective, focusing on ethical development, and fostering collaborative and global approaches, we can guide AI towards creating a future that is beneficial, enriching, and equitable for all.

AFTERWORD BY ONESIMUS MALATJI

My journey through the ever-evolving landscape of technology and innovation spans over 27 years, a period marked by remarkable transformations from the early days of the 386DX computers to the latest technological advancements. My experience encompasses a wide range of domains, including graphic design with tools like Corel Draw, newspaper publishing, and the intricacies of telecommunications, particularly in APN and networking via SIM cards.

This extensive journey in the world of IT has not only been a testament to my adaptability and continuous learning but also stands as a solid foundation qualifying me to impart knowledge as a teacher or lecturer. My expertise, honed over nearly three decades, encompasses both the technical and conceptual facets of technology, giving me a unique perspective on its evolution and impact.

My goal, rooted deeply in my passion for technology and its potential to transform lives, is to bring about a global change in humanity. I aim to achieve this through writing and speaking, channels that allow me to reach and inspire a broad audience. By sharing my insights, experiences, and understanding of technology, I hope to ignite a similar passion in others — to help them see the possibilities that technology holds for improving our world.

The journey through technology is not just about understanding machines and software; it's about grasping how these tools can be leveraged to make a meaningful difference in our everyday lives and society at large. It's about envisioning a future where technology is used not just for economic gain but for societal benefit — a future where technology serves as a catalyst for positive change.

As we stand on the brink of a new era dominated by technologies like AI, my mission is more relevant than ever. I am committed to guiding others through this complex landscape, helping them to understand, utilize, and ethically integrate these technologies into various aspects of life. Through my teachings, whether in a classroom or a public forum, I aim to empower individuals and communities with the knowledge and skills needed to navigate and shape the future of our digital world.

In conclusion, my journey in technology and innovation is more than a personal narrative; it's a call to action for others to join in this fascinating voyage. By sharing my knowledge and experience, I aspire to inspire a new generation of thinkers, innovators, and leaders who will harness the power of technology to create a better, more equitable future for all.

~~~~~~~~~~~~~~~~~~~~~END~~~~~~~~~~~~~~~~~~~~~